Silly Sketcher

Draw Silly Superheroes!

written by **Luke Colins**

illustrated by Catherine Cates

**BLACK
RABBIT
BOOKS**

Hi Jinx is published by Black Rabbit Books
P.O. Box 3263, Mankato, Minnesota, 56002.
www.blackrabbitbooks.com
Copyright © 2020 Black Rabbit Books

Jennifer Besel, editor; Catherine Cates,
interior designer; Michael Sellner, cover designer;
Omay Ayres, photo researcher

Library of Congress Cataloging-in-Publication Data
Names: Colins, Luke, author.
Title: Draw silly superheroes! / by Luke Colins.
Description: Mankato, Minnesota : Black Rabbit Books, [2020] |
Series: Hi jinx. Silly sketcher | Audience: Ages: 8-12. | Audience: Grades: 4
to 6. | Includes bibliographical references and index.
Identifiers: LCCN 2018025780 (print) | LCCN 2019000284 (ebook) |
ISBN 9781680729566 (ebook) | ISBN 9781680729504 (library binding) |
ISBN 9781644660751 (paperback)
Subjects: LCSH: Superheroes in art—Juvenile literature. | Figure
drawing—Technique—Juvenile literature.
Classification: LCC NC1764.8.H47 (ebook) | LCC NC1764.8.H47 C65 2020
(print) | DDC 743.4—dc23
LC record available at https://lccn.loc.gov/2018025780

Printed in China. 1/19

Image Credits

Alamy: Matthew Cole, 2–3, 5; iStock: carbouval, 5; Shutterstock: anfisa
focusova, 19; Designer things, 20; Mario Pantelic, Cover, Back Cover, 3, 5,
12; Memo Angeles, Cover, 5, 6, 11, 15, 16, 20; Nickolay Grigoriev, 20; Olga
Sabo, 5; opicobello, 7, 15, 17, 19; owatta, 5; Pasko Maksim, Back Cover,
11, 23, 24; Pitju, 3, 21; Ron Dale, Cover, 1, 3, 4, 5, 6, 7, 11, 15, 19, 20 Every
effort has been made to contact copyright holders for material reproduced in
this book. Any omissions will be rectified in subsequent printings if notice is
given to the publisher.

Contents

CHAPTER 1

Be a Silly Sketcher!....4

CHAPTER 2

Put Your Pencil to
the Paper............6

CHAPTER 3

Get in on the Hi Jinx..20

Other Resources...........22

Chapter 1

Imagine a world full of superheroes. Super humans flying and blasting all over. Well, you can draw that world. And you can make it as crazy and silly as you want.

To be a silly sketcher, all you need is a pencil, some paper, and a funny bone. Draw a square here. Add some big hair there. Just follow the steps. You'll have super art in no time.

What You Need

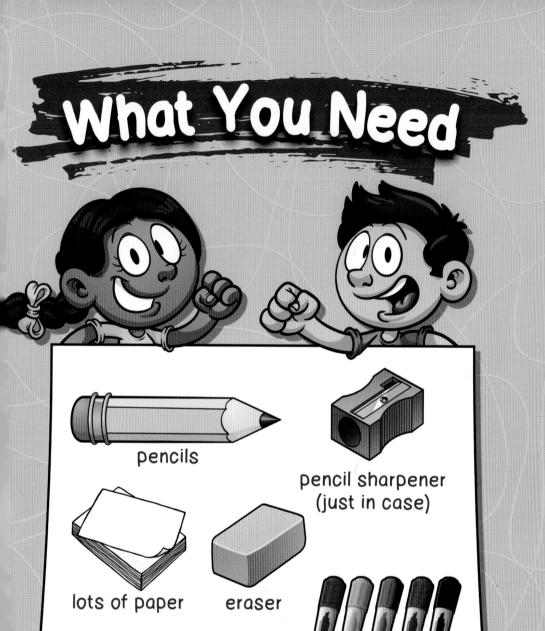

pencils

pencil sharpener
(just in case)

lots of paper

eraser

colored pencils and markers

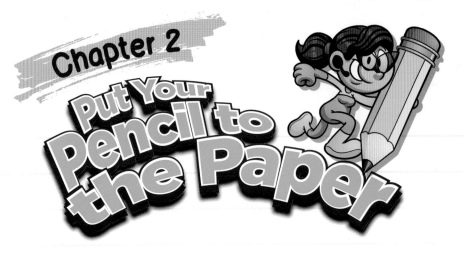

Chapter 2
Put Your Pencil to the Paper

Get the super-sized giggles going with this superhero. Making him look confused about his situation will make it even funnier.

Step 1

Start with a large oval. Then add curved lines to start the chin and hair.

Step 2

Give your hero big circle eyes, funny eyebrows, and a nose.

Step 3

Erase all the lines inside the **overlapping** shapes.

Step 4

Add **pupils**, a mouth, and chin details.

Step 5

Draw curved lines to make a mask.

Step 6

Add **motion** lines and **punctuation** to show the hero's confusion.

Finish It Up!

Use markers to **outline** your drawing. Then try colored pencils for shading it in.

Hopping Hero

Superheroes need super pets. Maybe this bunny has bouncing powers.

Step 1

Start the rabbit's body with a U shape. Use ovals for the head and ears.

Step 2

Add big eyes. Give the rabbit arms and legs too.

Step 3

Every super rabbit needs a cape. It also needs a nose.

Step 4

Erase all the lines inside the overlapping shapes.

Step 5

Add pupils, a belt, and wrist details.

Step 6

Add detail to the cape and shirt.

Step 7

Draw motion lines to make the cape blow in the breeze.

9

Big-Haired and Brave

This hero doesn't let villains stop her—even if she has to fly through trees!

Step 1
Use squiggly lines to start the hero's face and big hair.

Step 2
Add big eyes, a nose, and a mouth.

Step 3
Draw curved lines to add a mask and a headband.

Step 4
Erase all the lines inside the overlapping shapes.

Tip If you have trouble making the shapes, try **tracing** them first. Tracing is a good way to get a feel for how to draw something. Then try it on your own.

Step 5

Curved lines make the hero's body and cape.

Step 6

Add simple arms and legs. Put details on the eyes too.

Step 7

For fun, add leaves and sticks coming out of the hair. Draw in motion lines too.

Fireman Freddie

What would a hero who can make fire do? He'd heat things up! (That's a terrible joke. Sorry.)

Step 1

Start the hero's head, neck, and body.

Step 2

Draw on face features, arms, and legs.

Step 3

Give your hero some protective gloves and boots.

Step 4
Erase all the lines inside the overlapping shapes.

Step 5
Add details, such as a mask and belt.

Step 6
Draw motion lines and face details.

Step 7
Go wild with the flames. Have them coming out of anywhere you want!

Super Spin

This hero makes turning into a tornado look like fun.

Step 1

Use an oval and a twisted triangle to start the tornado.

Step 2

Add a head, eyes, and arms.

Step 3

Give your hero some awesome hair. Add two short lines for a neck.

Step 4

Add more ovals to make the tornado spin.

Finish It Up!

Try adding a background to your sketch. Maybe show a villain flying through the air!

Step 5

Erase all the lines inside the overlapping shapes.

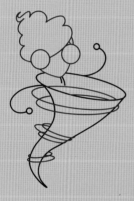

Step 6

Add more details to the face and tornado.

Step 7

Draw on details to the hair and face.

Step 8

Put in motion lines and flying leaves to really show this super spinner's power.

Jet Pack Problem

A hero with a jet pack would be pretty cool— until it starts on fire!

Step 1

Start the hero's face, body, and cape.

Step 2

Draw on some funky hair, a mask, arms, and a leg.

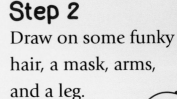

Step 3

Add two jets to the sketch. Give them some smoke clouds.

Step 4

Draw on some big eyes. Start a small fire on the cape too.

Step 5

Erase all the lines inside the overlapping shapes.

Step 6

Add details to the jet pack, including the controllers.

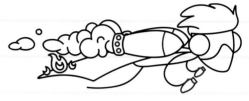

Step 7

Give your hero a worried **expression**. Finish the hands and foot too.

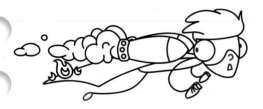

Step 8

Complete the sketch with a few more detail lines.

Hip-Hop Helper

This hero can dance enemies into jail! (Or maybe she's just celebrating. Your call.)

Step 1

Start with an **hourglass** shape. Then add a swooping cape around it. Draw a teardrop head too.

Step 2

Add a V shape inside the head. Put on arms, legs, and a neck too.

Step 3

Give the hero a cool mask and face features.

Step 4
Erase all the lines inside the overlapping shapes.

Step 5
Draw on details to the mask and uniform.

Step 6
Give the hero gloves and boots.

Step 7
Add details, such as buttons and an **antenna**.

Step 8
Make the hero boogie with lots of motion lines and music notes.

Tip Color your hero however you'd like. Maybe her suit would be funnier with polka dots.

Chapter 3
Get in on the Hi Jinx

Comic book artists use the same steps you just did! They use simple shapes to build the frames of their superheroes. Then they add details, such as shading and color. Maybe one day you'll draw for a comic book!

Take It One Step More

1. Most of the drawings tell you to erase the lines inside overlapping shapes. Why is that step important?

2. Are your sketches more or less funny with color? Why?

3. What features make these drawings funny?

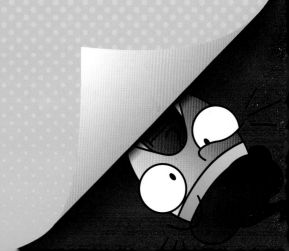

GLOSSARY

antenna (ahn-TEN-uh)—a metal rod for sending and receiving radio waves

expression (ek-SPREH-shun)— the way someone's face looks that shows emotions and feelings

hourglass (AHWR-glas)— an instrument for measuring time in which sand runs from the upper part to the lower part of a glass container in an hour

motion (MO-shun)—an act or process of moving

outline (AHWT-lyn)—to draw a line around the edges of something

overlap (oh-vur-LAP)—to extend over or past

punctuation (punk-shoo-AY-shun)—marks that are written to clarify the meaning of a sentence, such as a period or comma

pupil (PYU-pul)—the part of the eye that lets light in; in people, it's the round, black part of the eye.

trace (TRAYS)—to copy something by following the lines or letters as seen through a transparent sheet on top

BOOKS

Johnson, Clare. *How to Draw.* New York: Dorling Kindersley Limited, 2017.

Let's Draw Animals with Crayola! Crayola. Minneapolis: Lerner Publications, 2018.

Nguyen, Angela. *How to Draw Cute Stuff: Draw Anything and Everything in the Cutest Style Ever!* New York: Sterling Children's Books, 2017.

WEBSITES

Drawing for Kids
mocomi.com/fun/arts-crafts/drawing-for-kids/

How to Draw
www.hellokids.com/r_12/drawing-for-kids/

How to Draw Archive
www.artforkidshub.com/how-to-draw/

TIPS AND TRICKS

Make sure to let the marker outlines dry before coloring in your drawings.

Colored pencils are a great tool for coloring in your drawings. Layer a color over another for a cool blended effect.

Can't draw a straight line? Try using a ruler or other straight edge.

Don't worry if your drawings don't look exactly like the ones in this book! Art is all about creating your own thing. Just have fun!